It's All In God's Timing

"My Testimony"

Darlene Johnson

It's All In God's Timing: My Testimony

ISBN-13: 978-0-578-66927-4

Book design:
Williams DocuPrep
www.williamsdocuprep.com

Contents

Dedication

This book is dedicated to every person who struggles with their identity and feels that they have yet to walk into their destiny.

Acknowledgments

I would like to thank Carolyn Shepard, Bishop C. C. Dixon, Shareece Dixon, Prophetess Vernell Gore, and Shabach Ministries for their constant encouragement and prayer.

Thank you Pastor Kimberly Walker you have been encouraging and a great inspiration to me also.

With love,

Evangelist Darlene Johnson

God's Will

"The Lord is not slack concerning His promise; as some men count slackness; but is longsuffering to us-ward, not willing that any should perish, but that all should come to repentance." (2 Peter 3:9)

In the scripture above Peter is describing the sovereign God's desire that all people should turn to Him, and turn away from unprofitable lives.

Christ died for the sins of all mankind, but only those who believe, receive the benefits of that sacrifice. God's desire is for our salvation and growth in the truth, (sanctification) so we will not be led astray by false teaching. Lord, let Your will be done in my life on earth, as it is in heaven.

Living in the will of God is sometimes a challenge because we don't know the unknown. It is in His will that we can have life more abundantly. If we study and believe His Word, we can change to become what He wants us to be. He will not force us to live in His will, we must be willing to change, and trust Him at His word.

We know when we do wrong, yet we often do what we know is wrong. However, God is so merciful and loving that He forgives us over and over. If the Lord punished us for all the wrong we have done, we wouldn't be here. We should be grateful that He gives us chance after chance to repent of our ungodly ways. We need to ask the Lord to help us live according to His will. Father, give us the strength to do Your will.

We don't know when our time is up, so we should seek Him while we can. How do we seek Him? We seek Him when we set our hearts and mind on Him. We seek Him when we seek His and do what it takes to live according to His will. He reveals His will to us in His word, so we must read and study His word to find out His will.

Seeking is making an effort to get through the natural means to God himself—to continuously set our minds toward God in all we do, to direct our minds and hearts toward Him through the means of His revelation. This is what seeking God means.

This Is My Season

In my book, *"God Ain't Thinking What You're Thinking"* I stated that the Lord blessed me with a job in January 2011, which closed four months later. I continued to pray and look for other jobs. God certainly knew when He gave me the job that it would close in a few months. I understood this so I kept believing that God had a plan.

When I went to one interview, the secretary told me I was wasting her time. I continued to apply for jobs. I enrolled in Virginia College to study medical office administration in the summer of 2011 and was doing great.

Then, I was in a head-on collision in November 2011. I thank God I did not have any broken bones. When I went to the hospital, I found out I had whiplash. To God be the glory. I praise Him for keeping me alive.

The police report stated that I had pulled out in front of the other vehicle. This was not the truth, so I sent a letter to the police department in Jackson, Mississippi to explain exactly what happened. Even when the enemy went against me to imply that I was at fault, God gave me favor and set the record straight.

When you know that you have done nothing wrong, stand up for yourself and don't forget to pray. I asked the Lord to fix the situation, and He did. It wasn't long before He provided me with transportation because He said that He would "supply all of my needs." Trust God, whatever happens, He will turn your mourning into joy if you believe and don't give up.

In January 2012, I applied for the work-study program. While waiting to see if I qualified, I continued to search for work. When I was told that I was qualified, I talked to the coordinator. He said that I needed to fill out another background check form, and that it would only take a few days to check.

I waited and checked back with them, but it had not come back. Then, I was told that I needed to fill out another application because the one I filled out had gotten misplaced.

I went to the Student Services Coordinator about my background check. She checked into it and found that the coordinator had hidden my paperwork to keep me from being hired. God stepped–in and I started work as a library assistant.

Sometimes the enemy holds up your blessing, you must not give up on what you want to do. Be persistent. If you give up, you will miss your season. If I had not been persistent, I would not have gotten the job.

"Ask, and it shall be given you; seek, and ye shall find; knock, and it shall be opened unto you; for everyone that asketh receiveth; and he that seeketh findeth; and to him that knocketh it shall be opened." (Matthew 7: 7)

Since I moved to Biloxi, Mississippi, God has opened doors that I couldn't imagine would be opened to me. I am so grateful that I moved in His timing. Some would say, "well if you would have stayed still, He would have done it for you here." I haven't forgotten that He blessed me in North Carolina. It was a hard struggle when I was there, but it feels different here. I have peace.

Just as Jesus fulfilled His duty to the Father by dying on the cross for our sins, it is our duty to obey God. We must yield our will to God's will, and when you obey God to the fullest, He makes things easier for you. I don't mind waiting for the Lord to bless me because I know that when it's time, I will be blessed. So, I remain peaceful and joyous, knowing that He is faithful to His promised. If we patiently wait on the Lord to bless us, He will give us more than our heart's desire.

I was in three accidents and the Lord blessed me to come away with no broken bones or internal injuries. God kept me because it was not my time. I praise God because He allowed me this opportunity to tell others who are alive and well to give Him the glory, honor and praise, because you're still here.

I didn't have a car for nine months. God provided me with transportation to go where I needed to go without any problems. When my roommate went back to North Carolina, I asked God to bless me with my own transportation before she left, and He did. God will give you favor if you do what He says. His word does not change.

I asked the Lord to work a miracle for me, in a situation I knew wasn't right. I promise you He worked it out for my good. I truly thank Him for blessing me repeatedly. I am fully persuaded that there is nothing in my past that I desire to go back to. I'm happier than I've ever been because of Christ. I am sold out to the Lord. "NO ONE IS GREATER THAN HE."

When things go wrong in your life, pray, and give God the glory, because it could be worse. Give Him thanks for all things. I didn't give up. I continued to press my way through the pain, the disappointments, and the struggles, and God granted me mercy, love, peace, and happiness.

God has a specific time to do things for us. We may work hard to get the things we need or desire, but it takes time to get it. Sometimes we're unable to get it due to unforeseen circumstances. Sometimes it can take years, and even longer, to achieve our goals. It is surely in God's timing.

Sometimes we make plans and forget about our Savior Jesus Christ. We don't include Him in our plans. It is all about us, and what we want, but then we have a hard time getting what we want. We ask the Lord, *"Why am I having such a hard time obtaining what I need?"*

After the Lord has blessed us with our health and strength all week long to complete our daily tasks, we forget to pay our tithes and offering.

> *"Even from the days of your fathers ye are gone away from mine ordinances and have not kept them. Return unto me, and I will return unto you saith the lord of hosts. But ye said, wherein shall we return?*
>
> *(8) Will a man rob God? Yet ye have robbed me. But ye say, wherein have we robbed thee; In tithes and offerings. (9) Ye are*

cursed with a curse; for ye have robbed me, even this whole nation.

(10) Bring ye all the tithes into the storehouse, that there may be meat in mine house, and prove me now herewith, saith the Lord of host, if I will not open you the windows of heaven and pour you out a blessing, that there shall not be room enough to receive it". (Malachi 3: 7-10)

We have been bought with a price which JESUS paid on the cross, that we may live and have abundant life in Him. All He asks us to do is obey His rules. Once you learn the way of the Lord, you wouldn't want to live the way of the world.

I thought living for the Lord would be easy. Truth is, giving up my sinful life to live a life pleasing to the Lord was hard. I didn't think I could give up the old lifestyle which was killing me.

Changing my thinking was a was a process. I thank God that He gave me a strong desire to study His word. When I sincerely searched the word of God for myself, and continued hearing the Word preached and praying without ceasing, I fell in love with Jesus, even the more. Why? It was because in Him I found a new life, one I had never experienced before.

Disobedience

When I stepped out of the will of the Lord, my little world started crumbling down. When I came to my senses, I realized it was better for me to obey God and stop sleeping around, rather than acting like I had everything together.

We tell our children to obey us and to do good. When they disappoint us by not obeying what we tell them to do, we chastise them or spank them. That's the way the Lord is about His children.

When He tells us to do something, and we want His blessing, we have to do it.

You might remember the story of Jonah. Jonah refused to follow God's instructions and got in big trouble. God asks him to go to Nineveh and tell the people there to stop being so prideful and acting like heathens. Jonah refuses and runs away. He jumps on a ship heading for Tarshish.

While he is at sea, a terrible storm comes, and Jonah is thrown into the sea. The Lord caused a great fish to swallow up Jonah. Jonah was alive within the fish for three days and three nights. Jonah cried to the Lord, and the Lord caused the great fish to throw up Jonah on dry land.

Instead of doing what we are told; knowing the Lord has spoken to us to do it, like Jonah, the rebel we refuse. After the Lord saved him, Jonah went to Nineveh and preached the word to the lost souls as the Lord told him from the beginning.

I know that we wouldn't want this to happen to us. So, let us obey the Word of God, with all our hearts, soul, and mind. The number one decision we need to make is to obey the Word of God and its entirety. If we don't, we will suffer the consequences.

Don't make sacrifices that will cause you to lose out with God. Obey Him no matter what's going on in your life. Trust Him, don't doubt, and don't be anxious. Pray instead of giving up, and making unwise decisions.

When we disobey the Word of God, you can look for things not to work out the way you have planned. Why? "Because God is a jealous God," You should put Him first in your life, because without Him you can't really make it.

Sure we will get some things, but the struggles you will have in getting them because of our disobedience are not worth it. However, when you and I put people and things ahead of Him; watch things slip through your fingers, relationships failed, sickness comes, families at war with one another.

"My sons forget not my law; but let thine heart keep my command-

ments: (2) For length of days, and long life, and peace shall they add to thee. (3) Let not mercy and truth forsake thee: bind them about thy neck; write them upon the table of thine heart:

(4) So shalt thou find favor and good understanding in the sight of God and man. (5) Trust in the Lord with all thine heart; and lean not unto thine own understanding.

(6) In all thy ways acknowledge him, and he shall direct your path. (7) Be not wise in your own eyes: fear the Lord and depart from evil." (Proverb 3:1-7)

Don't allow Satan to keep you from fellowshipping with other Believers and worshipping at the house of the Lord. Stop making excuses about why you don't attend church. Stop blaming the Pastor, the congregation, or your family members. When Jesus comes for you and me, what excuses are we going to tell him?

Most of the time, when we call on the Lord, it is when a big disaster has taken place, or our loved ones have died. Let us come together when there is no disaster. Let us start now to pray for one another in season and out of season.

Obedience

"It shall be health to thy navel, and marrow to thy bones. Honor the Lord with thy substance, and with the first fruits of all thine increase. So, shall thy barns be filled with plenty, and thy press shall burst out with new wine" (Proverbs 3:8-9)

God promises if we obey His Word that He will heal us and strengthen us when we are sick. He will bless us to be healthy when we eat the right foods. He blesses us as we go out, and when we come in. God is good to us, and we owe Him a right now praise.

> *"The Lord shall command the blessing upon thee in thy store-houses, and in all that thou settest thine hand unto; and He shall bless thee in the land which the Lord thy God giveth thee." (Deuteronomy 28:8)*

This means to give unto the house of the Lord. If we pay our tithes and offerings, we will be blessed. When we don't give our part into the house of the Lord, why should we expect the Lord to help us?

We give our money to other people or purchase things we don't need, how can we go into the house of the Lord and ask for help when we didn't contribute when we were able? Is it fair for others to pay their tithes and offering and you don't? Now you need help from the church because you feel like they are supposed to help you, being Christians.

Well, if you would invest in the house of the Lord, you could get help. However, when the Lord blesses you to get on your feet, you tell yourself 'I know I promised to go to church' but you continue to do what you used to do. The Lord is watching every move we make. God loves us so much that He wants the best for His people.

"(11) My son, despise not the chastening of the Lord; neither be weary of His correction: (12) For whom the

Lord loveth He correcteth; even as a father the son in whom he delighteth. (13) Happy is the man that findeth wisdom and the man that getteth understanding. But it shall come to pass, if thou wilt not hearken unto the voice of the Lord thy God, to observe to do all His commandments and His statues which I command thee this day; that all these curses shall come upon thee, and overtake thee." (Proverb 3:11-13)

Why continue in the way of the world, and suffer? I've learned to obey the word of God, and ever since then my life has been great. Seriously, the Lord has given me wisdom and understanding about how to love Him first, and whatsoever I need He will supply. I'm telling you that God will take care of you in such a way that you will want to kick yourself for being out in a world of sin.

My body feels greater than it has felt in years. I won't take anything for my journey with the Lord. Nothing can compare to Him. As the song goes; I searched all over, I couldn't find nobody, greater than our God. I looked high and low, yet I haven't found anybody, greater than Him.

If you are reading this book, please obey the Word of God. Don't let life pass you by without getting to know who God really is. Give Him an opportunity to take care of you by obeying His precious

Word. "Study to show thyself approved unto God, a workman that needed not to be ashamed of rightly dividing the word of truth." He is worthy to be praised. He loves us all. He does not want us to perish. He wants us to obey His Word, and live holy for Him.

Everything will work out in God's timing, just trust Him and see. When I wrote my first book, I didn't know how it would turn out. I didn't know where I would get the money to publish it, but God made a way. I didn't know where to find a publisher, or who to talk to about what I should do. But the Lord allowed me to search the website, and I found a publisher that gave me a great deal for my book.

When my friend finished editing, I was excited about having a book to publish. I couldn't believe little old me could do such a thing! We never know what we can do through Christ Jesus, He allows us to do some great things if we put our trust in Him.

After the book was published, I prayed that it would go viral, and the Lord blessed the book to do just that. So, you see, if the Lord did that for me, what do you think He will do for you when you obey Him. I trusted the Lord because I know that He knows what's best for me.

I will always trust Him no matter what comes or goes. He has always been by my side when I didn't know that He was there. I love Him so much that I'm constantly thanking Him every day for all that He has done and is doing right now in my life.

Don't Kid Yourself

What I mean by that is, you may fool me, but you sure can't fool God. He knows if we are lying to Him when we say, "I promise Lord if You get me out of this mess I won't do it again." Who are you fooling? Don't kid yourself about God. He knows everything about us.

When we make God a promise we need to fulfill our promise to Him because if we don't when He pours His wrath upon us for being disobedient, no one can stop Him? Don't you see the handwriting on the walls? Look at the tornadoes, hurricanes, snowstorms and the devastating lighting strikes, fires that are hard to extinguish, land and houses being swept away through all the storms.

God knows us from the inside out. He formed us in our mothers' wombs, and then He gave us knowledge and an understanding of how our body is to operate. He allows us to go to school to learn how to read and give us wisdom and understanding to take care of His Temple, which is the body.

He blesses us with doctors to operate and when the doctors have done all that they can, God steps in and works a miracle for us. The Lord has blessed us abundantly where other countries are going through horrible times, and yet we still can't get along.

God is fed up with our grumbling and complaining about what we don't have when others have less. Since we do not appreciate one another or do what He tells us to do for one another, He's going to destroy us because of our disobedience.

You may not see Him in the natural, but you see Him in His work through the storms, tornadoes, hurricanes, and drought. God loves us, but He is a jealous God.

"(For the LORD thy God is a jealous God among you) lest the anger of the LORD thy God be

kindled against thee, and destroy thee from off the face of the earth." (Deuteronomy 6:15)

When we put things and people ahead of Him, He does not like that. I loved my family and other people more than I had realized. I thought I was indispensable, I could do anything, and I was available to help anybody when they needed me. I was old faithful, but I forgot about God.

I didn't worship Him when I needed to. I thought I was on top of the world; however, I soon found out that I needed the Lord to help me. I got tired, weak and weary.

Nothing seemed to go right for me. I was just going through the motions. I felt like a zombie, keeping busy and not listening to the voice of the Lord, and not studying His Word. My friends, let the Lord lead you and guide you in the way that He wants you to go. If you do this, life would be easier than you think.

I didn't realize how important the Word of God was to me. If you don't do anything else in your life, get the Word of God in your life. We need to willingly seek His presence in everything we do, which means that you submit everything, and everyone in your life to the guidance and will of Jesus Christ. That is what it means to acknowledge Him in all your ways.

A lot of things we ask for are not in God's will at the time, but it can come later in God's timing. Pray and ask the Lord to let His will be done in your life as it is in heaven. God has a perfect plan for our life if we seek Him for it.

When I turned my life over to the Lord and told Him to use me for His Glory, a change came over me. I am glad about the change. I read other spiritual books that inspire me to keep trusting in the Lord.

When I moved to Mississippi, I only knew my family, but I trusted God in the midst of my unfamiliar surroundings. God gave me favor with new people in my life. I had no idea that I was going to write one book, much less two books.

He will do the same for you. In His word, I remember reading about how to treat strangers because you may be entertaining angels unaware. So, God's Word will not return to Him void, He will take care of us when we do as He asks us to do.

Learn to lean and depend on Jesus, because He is our source of life, health, strength. He is our provider. Step out in faith, and trust the Lord, believe His Word, and don't doubt what He will do for you if you obey His Word. Learn to be patient, loving, kind, and especially thankful.

Treat your neighbor right, your enemies' right, and pray for the wisdom and understanding of God's Word, that you may live according to His Holy Word. God can do exceedingly, and abundantly above all that we ask or think. Why? Because He knows our thoughts before we do.

That's how awesome our God is. He is reliable; He doesn't lie, and He's the Keeper of our soul. Love the Lord with all your heart, mind, soul and body. God won't let you down. He surely has kept me all my life, through the good and the bad.

The Favor of God

When I was living in D'Iberville, Mississippi, not far from where I live now, I told the manager that I had written a book, and she asked me the name of my book. I told her *"God Ain't Thinking What You're Thinking."* I showed her a copy, and she offered to let me have a book signing at the clubhouse on the premises. I thanked her.

We scheduled to have it on March 30, 2012. Later I found out that she had moved, so I asked the new manager about it, and she said of course. It was planned before I came so you are welcome to have it here. I tell you the truth, God showed up and showed out for my first book signing. I really was happy that the Lord favored me that day.

I sent out postcards and flyers to my family and friends. One of my friends from North Carolina suggested that I contact the librarian to see if I could set up a book signing at the library.

I contacted her, and we set a date for June 7th. I went that evening and enjoyed an exciting and beautiful time! Out of all the years, I had lived there, this was my first time to have the pleasure of meeting the librarian.

God gave me favor that evening. I

had so much fun with my daughter and granddaughters. I told my daughter that when you do right God will bless you beyond your imagination. Since I've been back from North Carolina, I have had three more book signings. It was all in God's timing.

God has granted me favor with so many people, and I am thankful. When I needed another car, I thought my credit was so bad that I couldn't get a bank loan, so my sister and I prayed. Then I applied for the loan for the car and God gave me favor.

What I'm saying is, look to the Lord, He will give you favor if you obey Him. If you go to one place and it doesn't work out, keep trying, keep praying and keep believing until your breakthrough comes. He's given me favor at the bank, at college, with family, friends, and others. I am so glad that God favored me, and you.

I thank God for the plans He has for my life. I thank Him for how He thinks good things about me, and how He wants to give me a future in which He will be pleased. I'm waiting patiently for Him to work for me in His timing.

When the storm came through in August 2012, God favored me during the storm. I didn't have to leave my residence, nor was any damage done to the place where I was living. My lights didn't go out.

My sister asked me to come and be with her and my niece at the shelter where they were volunteers for the Red

Cross, but I didn't go because I trusted the Lord would take care of me during the storm, and He did. I felt it would be unsafe for me to go.

When the storms come into your life, and you don't know what to do, just fall on your knees and pray. Then allow the Holy Spirit to speak to you through the Word of God to direct you. If you don't know the Word of God, however, you can call on Him and ask for mercy.

When trouble came to my family, I prayed and interceded for my loved ones. I know prayer works for me. Sometimes we need to let God handle the situation because He knows best.

I prayed, "Lord, I know You know what's going on, and I trust You to fix it.

I can't be in two places at one time, but I know that you can. Lord, I thank You for solving the problem for me. Lord, help me be still while you are working on my behalf. I thank You for giving me peace about what's going on in my children's lives and my life. Amen."

When we give the Lord God our problems, we have to leave them in His capable hands and stop trying to fix them ourselves. He can fix it better than we can, because when we try to fix it ourselves, we make a mess of it. Then we call on the Lord and ask Him to help us when we should have called on Him in the beginning.

My daughter got sick after I moved to Mississippi, and I didn't have the money to go back home to see about her.

So I prayed and prayed to the Father about her health. I knew deep down inside that God would heal her in His timing. I prayed for her over the phone and encouraged her to pray, as well.

I asked her if she believed that God could heal her? She answered, "Yes, Mom, I do." So I asked if she believed in miracles and she answered, "Yes, Mama." I said, "It is according to your faith and I believe with you."

I kept in touch with her, praying and thanking God for her healing. She was diagnosed with vertigo, which made her so dizzy that she had to stop work and driving. I called her and told her I was coming home on June 9th, 2012 and that I would help her while I was there.

After arriving in Wilmington, North Carolina, she was scheduled to see a specialist concerning her condition. I took her to a specialist in Chapel Hill, North Carolina. They ran tests and told her they would notify her within two weeks regarding their rulings.

I prayed for her before I left to go back to Mississippi and I trusted the Lord for her healing. After two weeks she hadn't heard from them. She said, "mom the doctor has not called me yet concerning the test results." I knew then that God was working on her behalf. Finally, she called them to ask if they had found the cause of her dizzy spells, they had not found any!

I praise God for the miracle. Later, she went to the DMV and got her license. She's not working, but she is able to help herself better now. She cooks and cleans with help from her daughter. I owe God a right now praise. Hallelujah!

I love to pray for others because that's what we are asked to do. When I find out that someone is sick or in need, I prayed asking the Lord to fix the situation and to bless them and their family. I know what He can do because He has blessed me so many times when I was sick and in need. He is a present help in the time of trouble. You must believe in His Holy Word.

Every morning when I get up, I

realize that the favor of God is upon my life because I'm still alive and well. He gives me new benefits for the entire day. He covers me everywhere I go.

I praise Him for the blessing on that day. Each day is different and we don't know what will happen during the day, but God knows, and I'm glad about it!

Miracles Do Happen

My sister had to go to the hospital for a procedure concerning her heart in October 2012. Before she went, her daughters and I prayed that all would be well with her; that whatever was causing her to have heart palpitations, the Lord would heal her.

After the surgery, there was no blockage! I praise God for His faithfulness. God will take care of His people. The Lord is faithful and just, He will work miracles on our behalf if we just believe.

Whether we believe in miracles or not they happen. God works miracles every day. When I get up every morning and dress myself, that's a miracle; when I can breathe on my own without being hooked up to an oxygen machine, that's a miracle; all the things I am able to do in my daily life are miracles!

I haven't held a full-time job since September 2003. I know He has showered me with miracles. I haven't been without anything that I need because He supplies everything I need. He will do the same for you.

I dare you to trust Him for everything; I dare you to trust God. He will bless you if you obey His Word. Be faithful unto Him because He is faithful unto us. God will work things out in His timing if you will let Him. He knows our weaknesses, we can count on Him.

When I feel uncomfortable about a situation, I pray and ask the Lord to help me see things through His eyes so that I will not cause problems. I ask Him to help me understand what I need to do to resolve the problem that will be beneficial to me.

I ask God to keep me humble so that He can use me for His Glory. We will be tested, and tried, but if we keep the faith, trust God and faint not, He will bring us through those trying times. We can make it with His guidance and help.

When it comes down to our family, we are so quick to get upset and turn on God, blaming Him for everything that has gone wrong in their lives. Truth is, we bring things upon ourselves when we refuse to listen to Him, and insist on having our way.

We have this mentality that we are grown, and no one can tell us what to do until we get into trouble. We need to check ourselves and stop trying to have it our way. What do you or I profit from doing wrong? What have you and I gained when we refuse to listen to someone who knows how to be a blessing to us, and we dismiss their help.

Finding Peace

The ocean is where I find peace and serenity. Listening to the waves splashing, sounding like rain while the birds chirp as they fly by me is calming. I enjoy the cool breeze while I inhale the freshness of God as I walk along the pier, thinking how awesome God is to me. I close my eyes and envision Jesus walking on the water with Peter. I can't imagine what it would be like if I was walking on the water with Jesus. I know that there would be total peace and trust in my Heavenly Father.

I took a day and went to the ocean to just walk along the pier and spend some time with the Lord. While walking, I met strangers who stopped to talk to me as if we were friends. The word of God tells us to show ourselves friendly, and we will gain friends. I walked by a couple from Colorado and spoke to them as they looked out over the ocean. I praised God for a beautiful day as they spoke back to me.

Later, as I was walking back toward my car, a gentleman stopped me and said, "Miss, I don't know what you said to the couple, but you sure made their day." I told him I only said hello, asked how they were doing and wished them a wonderful day.

I praise God, even for the little things. I don't know if they had a problem or not, but that was none of my business. I'm glad that my speaking to them cheered them up. It surely blessed my soul.

Sometimes just a smile or a hug will help a person when they feel like no one cares for them. When I ask people how they are doing, some say, "fine thanks for asking." When we show love towards one another, we are doing the will of God.

Jobs

God has a job for us, but are we willing to work the job God has for us? Are we willing to give up our natural job and work totally for the Lord? I don't mean everyone should give up their jobs and become preachers because God needs people in the workplace as well as the pulpit.

My point is when we give up our desires and trust the Lord we shouldn't hesitate because He will provide for us and He knows what we need to do His work. Even though the job you are working may not be ideal, you have to be willing to work it until He promotes you to another position. Yet, we grumble and complain about our jobs when others are out of work and looking for a job to take care of their family.

While we are on the job we tend to do wrong, disobey the managers, and refuse to do what others were supposed to do. Then, if we get fired, we want to destroy the people or the place, when we had an opportunity to do the co-worker's job and get a promotion.

Sometimes God tries to promote us, and we say, no, I'm not going to do that because it is beneath me. If we would just humble ourselves, and let the Lord work in our favor, we could prosper and be successful right where we are.

Don't leave your job with an attitude, because it will be hard for you to get good references when you apply for another job. I went to college and I graduated. I applied for jobs in my field of study, but because I didn't have the experience, I was not hired; I was still looking. I sent resumes and filled out applications while waiting for an interview.

I asked myself, what does my resume for Jesus look like? What qualifications do I need to work for Him? Am I loving, forgiving, kind, gentle, faithful and understanding when I'm mistreated? Am I doing what He wants me to do to help others?

Am I studying His word more than doing what I want to do, or what others want me to do? Am I putting Him first in my life, obeying Him, meditating on His words day and night? Am I praying in season and out of season as He asks me to do? Is my resume lining up with His Word?

I believe if we search and research for Jesus and do His will, I know He will give us the job that will be pleasing to Him.

> *"Commit thy works unto the Lord, and thy thoughts shall be established." (Proverbs 16:3)*

An Overwhelming Miracle

As I continued to trust God for everything pertaining to my life, He worked a miracle in my life. In my first book, I stated that I would wait on God to bless me with a husband. In March 2014, I got engaged. On June 28, 2014, we got married. You see, God can do exceedingly, abundantly far more than we can ask or think.

While I was making plans to look for a job, God had a better plan for me because I promised to wait on Him. All of this was in God's timing. What I am saying to you my friend is let God be your guide. He will take care of you if you believe.

The plans I have made for myself didn't line up with the plans God had for me. That's why Isaiah 55:8-13 lets us know that our ways are not God's ways.

This is me and my husband. God blessed me with a loving partner. I am so thankful for what He allowed to take place in my life.

I told some of my relatives, and friends that I was going to wait for God to bless me. I was not giving up on God, because I knew deep down inside that He would give me my heart's desire. I didn't know when or where or how, but I was going to trust Him. He knows exactly what I need. He knows how to fix it for all of us.

God is great, and greatly to be praised. Not only did He bless me with a husband, He also blessed me with an extended family. I truly thank Him for my blessing. My family and friends were surprised and happy for me when I told them the news about me getting married.

My cousin said, "Doll you did say that you were going to wait and trust the Lord to bless you, and He did." Sometimes when we are trusting God for something and we tell people they don't believe us, but it's ok.

You must have faith in the Lord and believe that He will do what He says. I didn't have any doubt that God would bless me. I knew everything had to be in His timing. I didn't mind waiting because I knew that He would provide.

Everywhere I went God provided. I had to lean and depend on Jesus for everything. "Everything that happened to me that was good, God did it." After we got married, God blessed me with a job with benefits. I am grateful for what He has done in my life.

Whatever you do, don't give up on your dreams. Make sure you seek God for wisdom, understanding, patience and love. Forgiveness is the key to your success because when you forgive, then God can forgive you. Love and pray for those who are a little different towards you. Don't make it hard for them that don't like you, show them the love and kindness that God has placed in you.

Remember "God is love." When you seek God for anything you will have to wait and continue to fast and pray. Sometimes it seems like things are not going to change, but you must keep the faith. Look for it no matter what it looks like, just believe. All things will work out in God's timing.

God has allowed my blessings to overtake me in so many ways that I am more than excited, more than grateful, more than amazed, I am overwhelmed by His Love for me.

I take no credit for what He has done in my life. I will bless the Lord always; His praise shall continually be in my mouths, because of who He is in my life.

I'm making this prayer personally, because this is what Jesus means to me:

He is my Elohim, who made me, and crowned me with glory and honor. He is my El-Shaddai, the God Almighty of blessings.

He is the Breasty One who nourishes and supplies. He is all-bountiful and sufficient. He is my Adonai, my Lord and my Master.

He is my Jehovah – the Completely Self-Existing One, always present, revealed in Jesus, who is the same yesterday, today, and forever.

He is my Jehovah-Jireh the One Who sees my needs and provides for them. He is my Jehovah-Rapha, my Healer and the One Who makes bitter experiences sweet.

He sent His Word and healed me.

He forgave all my iniquities and He healed all my diseases. He is my Jehovah-M'Kaddesh. He's the Lord my Sanctifier. He has set me apart for Himself.

He is my Jehovah-Nissi, He is my Victory, my Banner, and my Standard. His banner over me is love. When my enemy comes in like a flood, He lifts a standard against them.

He is my Jehovah-Shalom, He is my Peace-the peace which transcends all understanding, which garrisons and mounts guard over my heart and mind in Christ Jesus.

He is my Jehovah-Tsikenu, my Righteousness. Thank you for becoming sin for me that I might become the righteousness of God in Christ Jesus.

He is my Jehovah-Robi, He is my Shepherd, and I shall not want for any good or beneficial thing. "Hallelujah!"

He is my Jehovah-Shammah, He is the One Who will never leave or forsake me. He is always there to comfort me and I am encouraged and can confidently and boldly say; the Lord is my helper; I will not be seized with alarm—I will not dread or be terrified. What can man do to me?

I worship and adore You, El-Elyon, you are the Highest God, who is the First Cause of everything, the Possessor of the heavens and earth. You are the everlasting God, the great God, the living God, the merciful God, the faithful

God, and the Mighty God. You are Truth, Justice, Righteousness, and Perfection. You are El-Elyon – the Highest Sovereign of the heavens and the earth.

I Still Have Joy

I was married for three years and four months, but then tragedy struck. My husband got sick. He was diagnosed with a stroke. They did a cat scan and found that he had blood clots on the brain. The medicine they gave him to dissolve the clots didn't help. He died, I was hurt, and I cried.

I am still hurting, but what keeps me going is that I know that he loved me, and I loved him. God blessed our marriage. We prayed together, traveled together, laughed a lot and enjoyed our family. He showed me how much he loved me and my children, grandchildren, and great-grandchildren. I will miss him terribly, but I know that God loved him best.

I thank God for the time we spent together. I won't forget when we went to church together because that was the best time of our life, serving the Lord together. That was awesome to have a husband who loved God and didn't mind going to church when he was feeling good.

He had love for whoever he encountered and had a special love for all babies. Every time he saw a baby, he wanted to hold it. They would just light up his life, and he would have a big smile on his face. I would laugh at the expressions he showed when he got near a baby. They would melt his heart. I enjoyed seeing him reaching out to play with the babies.

Our two-year-old granddaughter was his heartstring. When she came to visit, you couldn't ask him to do anything while she was there. He would pick her up, rock her, get on the floor and play with her and call her a baby. Then she would say, "I am not a baby because babies cry, Papa. I am a big girl." He would laugh and hug her, and they would play until he got tired.

I will always praise God for the gift He gave me, my children, my grandchildren, and great-grandkids. I know in life we will have trials and tribulations, but God is there for us.

I am not angry with God, because my husband died, but I didn't expect him to die that soon. He belongs to God, just like the rest of us. He allowed us to share three years and four months together, and it was wonderful.

I will cherish the time and places we went together. We had our disagreements, but it still turned out good. We learned that we were not perfect. Only Christ is perfect.

Some of his relatives would tease him about laughing so much. They would say, "it must be that woman you married", or "man I have never seen you smile like that before." I enjoyed cooking for him and I would make some of his favorite dishes like meatloaf, cabbage and blueberry crunch. We enjoyed hot fish with slaw, shrimp, and hushpuppies.

I will always miss cooking for him and all the love he showed me. He has two children and two granddaughters who he loved so much, even though he didn't get to see them as often as he wanted to. They, too, were his heart-strings. Whenever he saw them he was excited and gave them a hug. He loved all of his family, and really enjoyed everyone in his special way.

God Is Awesome to Me

In December 2018, my oldest daughter got into a bad accident. She needed surgery on her rotator cup. Then, she had to be transported to the ER, because she was having difficulty breathing.

After running tests they found that she had a seventy percent blockage to her heart. I praise God for His faithfulness! You see, God knew just how much I could bear. He blessed her to come through the operation and healed her. She is up and doing what she wants to do.

A few months passed, and the Lord blessed me with my own apartment. I am so grateful for what He is doing in my life. I could not have made it without Him being on my side. I thank Him for strengthening me in my time of troubles. I thank Him for my family and friends who supported me through all my trials.

After my daughter came home, I prayed and asked the Lord, what shall I do now? He laid Bishop Dixon on my heart to find him. I found his church, and called him and left him a message that I needed to see him ASAP.

God had an assignment for me to do, so I had to obey Him even though I had lost my husband. I still had to trust God, no matter what. I couldn't sit down on God because He is too good to me.

We expect God to do for us no matter what, but why can't we do what He asks of us. We must do like Job, continue to have a love for God. Job lost everything he had, and he still trusted God. When we lose a loved one, or whatever, we still must trust God.

I'm not saying that I understand why this happened to me. Who am I to question God? He knows everything about us, and how we're going to respond. That's why I pray and ask God to keep me humble and bless me to do what He has called me to do for His Glory.

I am not ashamed of the Gospel. I am so glad I answered the call to be an evangelist to help spread His Word. Whatsoever the Lord calls you to do for Him, do it. He loves all of us, but He hates the sin that we commit.

The Lord led me to Shabach Ministries under the direction of Bishop Carnell Dixon in Wilmington, North Carolina. We have worshipped the Lord together for years.

On July 28th, 2018, I was ordained as an Evangelist for God. My primary responsibility as an Evangelist is to preach God's Word, telling people simply and clearly what God says concerning His Son Jesus Christ and what He has done for us all. This is done with urgency because the souls of people are at stake.

The Evangelist is to be faithful to every word. We are not to just tell people about the Bible, we have to proclaim Jesus and communicate His message of salvation.

I am so blessed to be a child of the King of Kings and Lord of Lords. I wouldn't take nothing for my journey. This is the best day of my life! I am happy and honored to labor in God's vineyard. Oh, what a joy it is to Honor our Lord and Savior Jesus Christ.

Only God can do it. I am so glad that He favors me. I am glad for the teaching and preaching I've learned and heard over the years. I know that life is getting better for me because God is equipping me for my future with Him.

My mother has gone on to be with the Lord, but I thank God for her praying for me when I was much younger. I thank God for my family, friends, and loved ones for supporting me and for the prayers that went up for me unto God on my behalf.

I encourage you to trust in the Lord with all your heart and lean not to your own understanding. He can and will do exceedingly and abundantly far more than we can ask or think. What He has done for me and others He can do for you too. Trust in God for everything, it will work out in His timing.

Remember, He loves us and care for us. Don't stop loving God because things happen in your life beyond your control. Give thanks unto Him and bless His name. I wasn't expecting my marriage to end as soon as it did, but I thank God for my marriage because some said that no one wanted to marry me, but God made them out to be a liar.

When you ask God for favor and blessings, believe that He will do it for you; also wait patiently for it. Don't try to make it happen on your own. Wait patiently on Him, because He knows how, when, where, what, and whom He wants to bless you with. I trust Him with all my heart because He has performed many miracles in my life, and the lives of my family, and others.

I praise God for allowing me to be a part of Roseville and Shabach Ministries, and other ministries as well. I've learned a lot from the different places He has allowed me to go. I am not living by myself, but by His Grace and Mercy.

He is truly my everything. If He had not been on my side; I don't know where I would be right now. I am so glad that He loved me so much that He didn't allow the enemy to destroy me.

I am glad He chose me to be a vessel

for Him. Who wouldn't love an awesome God like this? I praise Him for what He has done for me and my church family, my personal family, and my friends. I really praise Him for everything. To God be all the glory, honor, and praise.

The blessings of God have made me rich. Let me tell you how awesomely my heavenly father provided for me. My husband passed away on October 28, 2017. Shortly thereafter, one of his children didn't want me to live in the home where we lived and I was told to vacate.

They gave my phone number to the ex-wife and had her call me. I told the woman to take out an eviction notice on me to be served so that I could leave, but she didn't. They didn't know that God had a bigger plan for my life and a better place for me to live. Psalm 37: 1 says, "Fret not thyself because of evildoers, neither be envious against the workers of iniquity."

I didn't pray for that person to be cut off, but I prayed that God would bless them. The word of God tells us to pray for our enemies and God's word tells me to bless and curse not, and that's what I did.

Philippians 4:19 says, "But My God shall supply all my needs according to His riches in Glory by Christ Jesus." Job 13:15 says, "Though they slay me, yet will I trust God."

I trust God because Jeremiah 29:11 promises, "For I know the thoughts that I think toward you, saith the Lord, thoughts of peace and not of evil, to give you an expected end." That means that He loves me and will not speak evil against me, He will give me hope and a future with Him, and no man can beat God.

I didn't leave because of what they had done. I believed God had something better for me. When your enemies come against you, don't fret. Keep doing what pleases God. He never fails. When you are going through hard times continue to seek God and praise

Him. He has all the answers that you need.

God blessed me with a home. When you help people and they turn their backs and lie on you don't try to get even with them. Remember the word of God says, vengeance is mine, and He will repay.

God told us to forgive so that He can forgive us. I'm so glad that I forgave my enemies. I thank God for who He is in my life. Don't miss out on what God has for you by not forgiving. Always keep praising, worshiping, and obeying God in your heart. Everything is going to work out in God's timing.

I pray that this book has inspired you, helped you, and encouraged you to trust in the Almighty God. No matter what the circumstance, or situation, God is all-powerful, all-knowing, loving and kind and He will strengthen you because He loves you and me.

Don't forget to fast and pray, study and meditate on God's word day and night. Spend quality time with Him, seek His face, pray His word to help you go through your trials and tribulations.

Lean and depend on Him for everything and have a personal relationship with Him. If I had given up on God, I don't know where I would be right now. Trust Him, especially when you don't know how things will work out for you. He knows what we need, but we must trust and believe, and obey Him.

He has great things in store for the ones that love and trust Him.

Hebrews 11:1 says, "Now faith is the substance of things hoped for, the evidence (assurance) of things not seen." Use your faith and trust God. Hold on to God's unchanging hand!

Loving you in Christ Jesus,

Evangelist Darlene Johnson

Made in the USA
Middletown, DE
29 December 2023

46334954R00053